I0884402

He Claims He Is the Direct Heir

HE CLAIMS HE IS THE DIRECT HEIR

LAZAR SARNA

The Porcupine's Quill

Library and Archives Canada Cataloguing in Publication

Sarna, Lazar, 1948–
He claims he is the direct heir/by Lazar Sarna.

Poems.
ISBN-13: 978-0-88984-282-3.--
ISBN-10: 0-88984-282-5

I. Title.

PS8587.A377H4 2005 C811'.54 C2005-903428-9

Copyright © Lazar Sarna, 2005.
1 2 3 • 07 06 05

Published by The Porcupine's Quill (www.sentex.net/˜pql)
68 Main Street, Erin, Ontario NOB 1TO

Readied for the press by Eric Ormsby; copy edited by Doris Cowan.
Typeset in Trump Mediaeval, printed on Zephyr Antique laid,
and bound at the Porcupine's Quill Inc.

All rights reserved.
No reproduction without prior written permission of the publisher except brief passages in reviews. Requests for photocopying or other reprographic copying must be directed to Access Copyright.

Represented in Canada by the Literary Press Group.
Trade orders are available from the University of Toronto Press.

We acknowledge the support of the Ontario Arts Council, and the Canada Council for the Arts for our publishing program. The financial support of the Government of Canada through the Book Publishing Industry Development Program is also gratefully acknowledged. Thanks, also, to the Government of Ontario through the Ontario Media Development Corporation's Ontario Book Initiative.

Canada Council for the Arts
Conseil des Arts du Canada

Canada

ONTARIO ARTS COUNCIL
CONSEIL DES ARTS DE L'ONTARIO

ACKNOWLEDGMENTS

The following poems have appeared in journals:

'Someone who has never seen' (1998, *Canadian Jewish News*), 'When he took his medicine' (1998, *Descant*), 'Herzl's Beard' (1999, *Descant*), 'Herzl's Beard' (1998, 7 *Parchment*), 'Police Blotter' (1999, *Descant*), 'The Will' (1999, *Descant*), 'Fiduciary' (1998, *Descant*), 'When the Fish Swallows' (1999, *Descant*), 'Final Notes on Progress' (1999, *Descant*), 'Because of the Peculiar Nature' (1997, *Antigonish Review*), 'Memo' (1997, *Antigonish Review*), 'The Treasure' (1997, *Antigonish Review*), 'The Treasure' (1999, *Descant*), 'Chronicles' (1997, *Antigonish Review*), 'He claims he is the direct heir' (1997-98, *Parchment*, 'The Veranda' (1997, *Prism International*), 'The Veranda' (1999, *Descant*), 'One Thousand Years of Jewish Spanish History' (1997, *Canadian Jewish News*), 'Back then she was a jagged top' (2001, *Canadian Literature*).

CONTENTS

HE CLAIMS HE IS THE DIRECT HEIR

He claims
he is the direct heir.

On the night of the revolution
as his family was being murdered
in the royal cattle stalls
he hid his tiny body under balls of manure
until long after the animals were stilled.

Delirious, hair stinking of clods
and seeping milk,
he fled the palace grounds into the forest, fell asleep with
whimpering rats in a hay field.

He grew to health
under a peasant's roof and
halo of retired flies.
He left one day
without expressing gratitude,
as was a king's prerogative.

Many years later
when it was known
he was alive abroad
there were detractors, reporters, runts
indistinguishable from true assassins.
He had no conclusive evidence
he was heir except
the scar, the details
of royal desserts, names of several butlers,
late visitors of his father
and wallpapers in rooms where he would dream.
Emigrés were convinced, and spoke in awe
to their children who, now and then,
chortled at their accents.

His wife believed until her death
he was the emperor
of universes
but bore no sons.

With her gone
and crushing news
both from his doctor and remorseless broker,
he announces now
from the window of his cottage
that in the seventy-eighth year
of his reign
all his palaces, running dogs, granaries
all his powers of law, of war, of fact,
all the wealth of his domain shall
revert to the masses
so misguided all these decades;
and may his father's soul
in its plenitude of majesty
find the ways and means
of forgiving those who served.

BECAUSE OF THE PECULIAR NATURE

I

Because of the peculiar nature
of the relationship with his staff
he would, before addressing them,
put on a mask full of eyebrows
and like a sedate reptile
give his orders of the day
through glazed and unflexed lips.

His blood
like the ink of a ballpoint
was not wet:
that dry quality
permitted him to
move through time and people
even though his living streams
had long stopped flowing.

II

He cared enough
once a year
to cross the border
where we waited
to transport him
deep into the city
past the buildings
we said were his,
past the factories
he thought were doing well,
past the mounds of accounts
and bonds
that could have been
in his name.

III

His middle name
Miriam
jabbed like a splinter
into his card.
His parents were right
to fear not bearing
a daughter
after six sons.

He is their unborn nominee
without power to fulfil.

WHEN HE TOOK HIS MEDICINE

When he took his medicine, he was normal;
when he didn't, his tongue would leap
from his mouth like a parachutist
held by one faithful vein that glimmered
profanities at his friends.

When he was crazy
his eyes, tethered revving motorcycles,
roared about his wife's pornographies,
her family's itch for money,
his children's unexplained diseases.
For their sake, we prowled where he prowled
using a box of bulging impatiens
as our camouflage.

When he took his medicine, he was so new
he came home without apology.
He would even make himself
a gourmet supper from brown leftovers
and call many times for his shredded slippers.

MEMO

Memorandum to death
not to occur
while we
berate garage men,
or pry at food in our teeth.

Make death not come
while we hold the line,
smile for a picture,
or paint part of the staircase.

Let there be no buttons missing from
our cuffs,
no bitten blemishes on
our nails.

Make sure the match reaches the cigar.
Protect, reserve, foresee.
Do not make death unwelcome.

WHEAT

Wheat fell from the sky
from a point above the spire.
I paid my housekeeper to gather and grind it
and bake a workable bread
to pay my debts.

The next day
I appeared with bowls and baskets in case
wheat fell again, which it did.
I kept coming day after day
till my dormers were full of kaiser rolls.
My housekeeper exhausted,
I put her on a train for her aunt's house.

The last day, the sky was tight-fisted,
coldly handsome, expressionless.
I stood by until a dog splashed me.
As I had more debts to pay
and no means of moving the sky to work,
I made idle talk with a man who wore a rich suit.

EVEN IN THOSE DAYS

even in those days
the interpreter of dreams,
if he was generous,
would tell whoever paid him
good would come;
but for non-payment
he foretold misery

the dreams were the same.

how could he be dishonest;
these were the only sacred visions
private people had

today ask any interpreter,
if you can get an appointment,
what will be,
and maybe several weeks after payment, he will answer:
what's a dream?

DOES SHE LET THE DOOR CLOSE

does she let the door close once she has passed
does she corrupt her stomach to make you look away
does she act as if she married her own kidnapper
does she let branches swing as she walks a path
does she leave windows open to the rain
does she toss a cigarette to burn down the ground
does she have your drink because she thirsts
does she break glass and abandon the shards
does she stain your clothes on her eating
does she disregard your dialogue for a gleam in her nails
does she talk faster when you heave a first snore
does she think of a cruise when you ask for a bandage
does she ever come back when you think she returns

SHE WANTS A HOTEL ROOM WITH A VIEW

she wants a hotel room with a view
of the cliffs cracking
at the scratch of waves
in a literature of scars

she wants a house with a view
of pines promulgating needles
throughout a valley
in a legislature of leaves

she wants an airplane seat with a view
of the sky terrific with clouds
spread contiguously
in a ligature of mist

she wants a face with a view
of complaints she scatters
over great surfaces
in a litany of rain

BACK THEN SHE WAS A JAGGED TOP

Back then she was a jagged top of a can toward her.
She made her grovel in every broken glass bowl
she could tear,
by making her cry haze-burnt, olive brine.

No way her son would live with
a person as thin as a shelf,
no way she would show at the wedding
but outside was good enough to scream angry old socks
as the bride left the hall
in white and confused confetti.

She was no good for her so young yo-yo.
The daughter-in-law smelled like cooking laundry,
and the tea always had a hair in it,
let alone the dirt piled up in an Everest in the kitchen.

Her babies were all born with soft heads;
why so many and who's going to pay for all of these piglets?
But they grew into scrap metal,
and in harmony always thought their grandma
was a crab or sharp conch.

When she became sick always,
and fat more than a moose,
and had to move in with them,
(her son sold pieces of trucks overseas
and had no time),
so instead of objecting, and not having grovelled for so long,
she said to his mother,
let me wash your back until you sleep,
and bring you
warm deep thimbles of eggshell soup.

MY DAUGHTERS SHOULD MARRY

My daughters should not marry anyone in that family.

Rather, a candlewick placer because of his patience,
and any man who has quick hands to catch small fish.

He might be a person who determines whether planks of wood
should be returned to the tree for further growth;
and whether reams of copper wire feeding an abandoned factory
should be stripped and melted into thimbles.

He might be taller than their shoulders or grow faster than they,
or he might always be lying down to see
if the house he builds for his wife will be forever stable.

He should have a very loud ability; but when he calls,
he should simply raise his tongue and then let it collapse.
For when he is close to his wife, he as a breather
should form part of the other breather.

But if they were to marry any in that family,
they would have torn bags of hot ash as husbands;
they would not know where to hide
from rains of insults, and unstopping metronomes;
and I as a father would be known in the streets
as one who lost his dignity and rescinded his own children.

NO ONE IS ACTUALLY ON THE SHORE

No one is actually on the shore
to greet sea-crashed men,
except the shore.

It is a warning
that the beach is a bad boy
unused to absent fathers.

They have come delirious and invisible.
Shrewd gulls poke
edges of the tide
like shopkeepers on a slow day.
They step onto shreds of kelp to shriek,
nothing to eat, no one to see,
no one to convince
and no guests to greet.

USE A CHAIN OF TAILS

Use a chain of tails to measure
wild paths animals take

Or use a chain of sticks to chart
where the next leaf feels like growing

Or use a chain of iron to trail
veins metals spread throughout the earth

Or use a chain of mushrooms to gauge
what moulders under satin grass

TWO BROTHERS

Two brothers followed wild cows into the grumpy forest.
The animals bared their gums and stiffened their udders
against a mossy breeze.

Then their faces, usually as accepting as a used frying pan,
showed off rainbows of angry wrinkles.

Their bovine wrath at each other so distorted their eyes,
they could not see the brothers hidden behind stacked salt cubes
and very frightened by the truth of how milk is made.

I MADE AN INCISION

I made an incision partway through my tie
with a one-edged mourning blade,
a surgical machete in a paisley field.

Next I looked for natural belly seams in a beef torso,
the white veins on banana meat,
anything that did not need my cutting,
the fault lines of topography.

Someone died.
But my rending my clothes is not proof.

Look at the bridge he used to cross every day:
it now blocks the water from passing
with its stilts and there may be a flood.

The shoes he used to wear walk from the closet
up to the roof where they rest like worn jays,
and they come back when work is over.

Look at the books he once ignored:
they now shake like a rag of wet dogs,
words fly off and land here on a diamond facet
and there in a meal of silences and seeds.

I cannot mend the rend;
of course torn things stay torn.
Bereavement ends tomorrow.

THE WILL

The vehicles
some with metal heart fatigue,
the apartments
some with bitter drains,
the bank boxes
some with sandy key shafts,
the vested suits
some with cross-eyed lapels,
are now the estate.

To you, for your brooding portfolio
to you, for your lapsed education
to you, for your foreign vegetables
to you, for your charities of summer
I leave what you deserve
lost in the wrinkles of
mortmain.

FIDUCIARY

She still keeps the letters
of her last lover
sealed in a box like
the meat of a nut secure in its walls,
sometimes on a white shelf
wide as the arms of an almond tree,
sometimes on the mantelpiece
by a bowl.

She knows I think
of ways to smash its casing,
see what keeps its freshness
through the years.

What will I find by espionage
by hinting to her
my jealous clues;
nothing but shells of shells
of eaten fruit.
What will I find in grabbing outright:
nothing but fires too small
for her needs,
but potent enough
to char my trust.

A THIEF OF DIARIES

A thief of diaries usually piles his cache
on a wilderness floor to burn on cold nights,
fuelled by moss and owl's eyes.

Personal anguishes
also help to spark and crack dry pine rockets
upward
into a black and private heaven.

LIVE CHICKENS

live chickens stacked in grid cages
on an open abattoir truck heading to east-end Montreal
feel the freedom of the highway air fluffing up
their genuine white plumage,
enjoy with a thousand full blinks
through their poultry brains
what a thrill it is to
ride and cluck

free as a floppy comb
free from a pecking crowd
free from chicken dictators burnished
with bold thighs and beaks,
free to dream of eating
grains of salt in a mash of wheat
off a heavenly floor made of sawdust, cloud
and freshly pulled and slightly warm down

CHILDREN SLEEP

Children sleep
faces flying,
arms contoured by the art
of wetting and dreams.

So embedded in night,
they are below tree stumps,
below the last finger of roots;
so deep have they slipped
that clocks, having grown heads,
hood themselves and go
anonymously
to live in another dimension.

HE COULD NEVER PROVE

He could never prove he loved her
just by hauling pine trunks over wools of moss.

A faulty axe that chopped with fibrous coughs,
he thought rough work was sincerity,
that she, like a timber counter, would give him credit
by the unit.

For seven years, until she hid away forever,
the smells she washed in were never thyme
or the musk of rock and twig slugs,
but sweet starch and vine roses
and tendrils of hay that would weave into a skirt.
Her hair was talcum,
the light spread of freckle, lily pollen.

His last and softest embrace of her,
the longest she permitted,
was a wrap of gravel wedges warmed in the brief winter sun.

The days sharpened without her cold lip.
He complained too often of the raw of his cedar throat.
The spaces between his teeth and joints stretched;
he became too loose, his root too shallow,
to grasp hard handles and new complexions.

THE TREASURE

We lost a week arguing with navies
and the sons of skeletons we might find.

Ropes fixed to the hull,
the last drowned cry of fifty years
was dragged up like the water's iron tibia.

Inspectors wanted to see our permits:
who gave you the right to reclaim
handprints on the deck rails
and silverware sprouting fins.

As we quarrelled, water drained from the ship
like fluid from a hanging cow.

We picked at the treasure
until it lifted from its vegetation.
With our law and bank prevailing,
we left for outside seas.

Behind, in our undertow,
every fish, from those with terrorizing tongues
to those with funny bladders,
asked about the hulk's most secret misery.

THE LARGE FIREMAN

His neglect to fix his own stairs
led us to buy the plank,
and even install it
for the overblown leg of
his pregnant wife,
for the celery-stalk legs
of his several kids,
for the vein-blackened legs
of his mother-in-law
and for his own white legs
that took such things for granted.

Years after he left
the fire department
(too heavy to climb the ladder)
he realized
each day brings new fires in
tiny windows
that will not permit
even the smallest of men
to help those
most in need.

UNDER THE GARDEN

Under the garden of bones
at Head-Smashed-in-Buffalo-Jump
breath seeps up
like a constant message from earth;
a crushed bison planted sideways
smelling of cow gums
and hairy musk
inhales the soil it is part of,
exhales its own calcium.

The roar of legs of hunted meat
hangs like
a phantom of sound
where dust used to be.
The eyes of generations of broken necks
have turned to cobblestones.
They see the herd
was a living trap,
because the only thing they could have done
while hurtling
over the cliff was to
wait.

DOORMAN TO THE STARS

I open the door to let you soar ahead
like comets' wind.
My palm is shaped much like
the holes of heaven, quiet humourless suction
for quarters, dimes.

The door, what majesty of
grace it has, both in its
coming and prophetic closing.
I am a muscle
of a strong angel's wing.

GRILLES IN THE WINDOWS

Grilles in the window finally
yanked, sawed
or mutely dissolved;
in any case,
no longer there.

But there are still
lines on your onions,
threads running the bananas,
lettuce grilles and veins;
I am moved by fear of confinement
to eat through everything
your salad describes so starkly.

Undone from our bouquet of jails,
we are burners for reform,
suggestive bubbles
in floating laundry;
our furniture peels new for us,
appetites broil our liberated menus.

It is our polite fingertips
pausing before impact
that find at least
one way of pardon.

I TAKE MY NAME

I take my name from the baker
bolting from the oven for a smoke
in the lane he sees through eyelids
dusted with future breads

I was named for that moment
when he transcends kneading

I take my name
from the dredger of rivers shutting his engines
to test a scared current.

I am named for the surprise he feels when his silt turns up
in potted plants.

My name commemorates when things break away
like the time miners of salt
forget what they drilled
cry out in their own tears and gravies.

THE PARTNERS RETIRE

That one grocery store
could support two partners
for thirty-five years
despite floods, spoilt fruit,
holdups and inspectors
was more amazing than they imagined.

They worked without a fight
and retired with the same old face.

No longer driven before lunch
to deposit the cash,
no longer concerned with rotating old stock,
they forgot each other
until in a dream, with one woken eye
on order from death,
they began to worry
whether the other had locked the door
on the very last night.

POLICE BLOTTER

I

By the bakery on the vague street
that shuns its own houses
the exchange between victim and thief
led from a no, to a yell
to a knife, to a fall.

For a few bills and a bag of light corn rolls,
I chased the assailant.
Slipping on a curl of blood
I faltered
then began with grace my cautious prowl
through the vicinities of fugitives
each of whom swore
he was never near the smell of bread.

II

The banker,
still raw from the terror of his robber
rose late
from a dream of revenge.
He somehow knew where to find
the vicious tattoo,
the face mask stained with hot breath.

There he trapped the criminal.
But he could only be surprised by the
dull reaction, absence of fury
in the robber's veins:
'I have desecrated, now I repent.'
Foreclosed by what he saw as insult
the banker left, moneybag lashed
to his heart.

On his return, the rawness gone
he watched over the bills
bound like families
each package crisper, neater than before,
stacked in the vault, and
warm in the steel
of the safest home.

III

Depending on where you stand
the firing squad is a team effort,
fresh air, rah-rah.

The fans, if any, go wild
in the last minutes of play
they rush to the field and grab
the lips of the victim while
over the melee hangs his lawyer's ominous question:
'Why is time, money?'

The air, the turf are cleared
particles of anguish taken away;
behind the stands,
beyond the walls
in black markets of enthusiasts
the search is on
for freshly minted crimes.

IV

The day after the stick-up
the manager could only shout
at the desperate crowd,
whimpering or cursing
through the plate glass doors,
that everything was under control.

But bonds, bracelets and
precious coins decorated
the bank floor
without any pattern or control.

It must have been an
inside job
maybe, just maybe the
manager himself;
why would he otherwise
be so reluctant to answer
any questions
or give back
diamonds cupped in his hands
to one old customer
who wet the queue.

SO LITTLE TIME

so little time
to pronounce all the diphthongs
or choose an accent in Esperanto,
to visit Venezuela after mountain rains
or walk on kernels of coffee beans,
to feel the starch float off the pasta,
to learn the music that wires feel
each electric time they jump.

so little time
to try on clothes for longish arms
and conceal a stomach in double lapels,
to bring birds into a room for a dialogue on air
and compare colours and make stripes and shades,
to salvage diamonds of tar in highways
and narrow the roads with mad white lines,
and record the chatter of new foods,
to bury the millions of broken umbrellas,
and light thin candles for their bent spokes.

so little time
to invent gadgets for a patent clerk
and see discovery annoy competition,
to buy watches for every occasion
and look at all their faces as an excuse,
to have visions of the end of days on cable
and not have them spoil the act of seeing,
to have the right change and need nothing
and give each story a house and patience.

PEEL OF A SAD CELLO

I choose to hold, or choose to throw away
the wife of old nails, and the wife of manicures
a son of strong hands, and one pinned to your pockets
an enemy with teeth of feathers, and one with a marble neck
candles with waxless bodies, candles with rusting wicks
a food of brick, a food of acid
a car that hums, and a car that collapses the driver
an office tower of napkins, and one built of torches
a star that works, and a star with a black other side
a teacher with castanets, and one that throttles books
a quick paymaster, and one that bends coins
a wave of salmon, and one that sprays your eyebrows
mites that lie in a ball, mites that strive for good diction
a chair that holds bottoms, and one with legs of spears
a candy of smooth crystals, and a candy of pure paint
a pant leg hiding a shoe lace, and one dripping salt
a horse on drums, and one that sleeps on its back

and a fruit of several pleasures, and a peel of a sad cello
an orange of a thousand sections, and a skin of dense bruises
a juice that runs from planets, and a pit that holds its sugar
a seed that makes its soil, and an earth that bites its roots
a sea so full of salad, and a sea of endless hunger

I DON'T LIKE YOU

I don't like you
I don't like the children you made for me
each leaving, or brushing only some of their teeth

I don't like you sleeping without working at it
you become part of the bed and yet your eyes,
which I hate, are fish eyes that dream

I don't like your mother
living half a melancholy life;
I don't like your father, a trapper of himself

I don't like searching for your buttons
at the bottom of a prickly sewing basket
I don't like you directing me
to follow the lines of your forehead

I don't like your voice masculine when shrill
unanswerable when soft,
I don't like you when I bite,
you trust me not to hurt

I don't like your preferences in poetry over mine
I don't like the breadth of your smile
when it's larger than my face

I don't like you counting my years
as your years of marriage,
we have our own ages and our selves as couples

I don't like you
I never have and never needed proof
I don't like you near me,
unless you agree to be me
I don't like you or anything in me like you

WHEN LOST

When lost in the forest,
plant your coins
in a thumb-deep grave,
test the mushrooms
by the fur of their undergills,
do not bathe in
the tail of the first stream you find,
calm the out-of-breath fear
of smart wolves' eyes

create fire
through the friction of your lungs,
learn that moss
is a community of green,
do not think landmarks
stay still for your directions,
eat only berries
that flies want,
reason you will have to stay
and there is room,
do not write messages on trees:
no one reads the trees

leave when you want, when you can,
imagine your way out,
believe it is not there
to hold you in, nor impress

EAT

eat the earth out of flowerpots,
your manners will be vacuumed;
eat the earth from under popular singers,
your gulp will be recorded;
eat the earth in construction sites,
your vision will be bulldozed;
eat the earth frozen under skis,
your frustration will be numb;
eat the earth stuck in tires,
your fear of moving flattens;

eat the earth at the feet of the Rockies,
your sight of the hawks improves;
eat the earth of Babylonia,
your dead from the Flood revive;
eat the earth of asteroids,
your willingness to fly
will find black holes

THE POOR HAVE CLAIM

The poor have claim to part of all my food,
whether I eat, or want to eat,
or throw it away.

But if it is an acrid after-growth of salad,
do they want to be entitled?
Or if it is a juice berry used only to dye,
do they think they can have the
colour off my fingers?

What if it is a cucumber look-alike,
but really a metal thumb unearthed in the fields,
is it part theirs?

Or if for a drunken reason,
I have to eat shirts, buttons, sizing, and plastic thread,
is it their food too?

Do my teeth have a duty
to chew only my portion?
When can I eat only for myself?

WE CANNOT HAVE FERMENTED GRAIN

We cannot have fermented grain: its rising disturbs us.

Nor crusted *kutah* that closes up the heart
because of the milk whey;

nor dyer's broth, which is bran water with pigment;

nor scribe's paste, which is also a toilet paste
used by the daughters of rich men
and left over by them for the daughters of poor men;

nor cook's dough, which is made from the flour of corn
one-third grown
and which absorbs froth when perched
on the lip of an open pot;

nor barley vinegar, which used to be hard wine.

THE MEALTIME OF GLADIATORS

The mealtime of gladiators and arena fighters
is the first hour;
we know that from their reactive chests
against the sunrise's white blades.

The mealtime of cursers and vandals
is the second hour;
we know that from their last night's chiplets
of blood on their socks.

The mealtime of inheritors
is the third hour;
we know that from the painful yawn
in changing lazy faces.

The mealtime of scholars comes later
because the logic of food is a long test.

Mealtime is the place for confronting body history.
A cream drop or shingles of fish make them all eaters.
In each of their hours they unite to strengthen their next hungry fear.
Otherwise they would have little in common
except their simple passage.

WITHOUT WHEAT

Without wheat, we can't chew the bran
into a warm paste to cover wounds;
we can't line hot water boilers
that are often out of control, with flattened grains;
we can't make miniature pastries
that float lightly in honey with raspberry kernels for colour;
we can't bring sheaths
like an armament to testify at harvest;
we can't feed cows that need rough field particles
and have strength thereby.

But it is dangerous to open Syrian round bread
without water in an open bottle nearby;
or to grab a barrelful of stalks to your chest
to squeeze out the dust in the wind;
or to scrape the back of a hand against a burlap sack of chaff
lying around as mouse bane;
or be in the same room as a wheat mattress recently used for dying
and never shaken and straightened to get rid of the form.

SOME BIRDS

Some birds have two wings of despair.

One dips its feather tips in varnish
and whacks the pillars of an underpass.

The other uses the beginnings of its elbow
to jab eyes out of apples on the tree,
or gawk at a mile-length of shopping carts wedged together
on a mall's tarmac.

When those wings fold away
like two sidesaddles,
birds are sullen royal consorts inspecting
an honour guard,
hands cuffed behind their backs.

I COULDN'T BE THERE

I couldn't be there because my new shoes were chewing my heel
and a pelican was yawning in my stomach where cramps spawn,
and my eyes were powdery and pink in the back.

And even had I gotten there,
my molars were reacting to cold like there were glass slivers in my gums
and I couldn't have eaten because my lungs
were turning into bags of cashmere lint.

Have I told you my hair felt inflammable?

And even if I had enjoyed myself,
I get so bloated when that happens, my toes grow spicules of excitement
and I ruin the socks you gave me;
how would you carry home someone
who looks and flops like mangled liver?

And even had I gotten home,
the cold radiators would have been running on slow clay
not to mention the loud neighbour
who is celebrating another wedding of a daughter
to the same masquerading lout everyone thinks has
much old money.

IN THIS PLACE

In this place,
all fruit waits to explode and injure,
all parcels are suspect,
all wine is poisoned.

No one stands near strangers,
all are strangers.

The face distrusts the back of the head,
the light is afraid of its filament.

There is no family.
There are gangs of one
ready to fight battalions of one.

It will change with generations,
when the first thought on waking
will not be ingratitude,
when the first shoes of the day
will have soft rubber pads
and smell of freshly diced hay.

I WAITED FOR YOU

I waited for you at the restaurant until
my elbows wore through the placemat.
I ate twenty-two packets of sugar wondering where you were.
The waitress didn't believe me, so I squeezed
the neck of the ketchup bottle into my mouth.

You forgot about me.

You wouldn't like the beans they serve here.
I counted them for you.

WE SEARCH HOLES

We search holes in walls between neighbours;
if too deep, or if a snake lives inside,
we go as far as our arm is safe.

We search book bindings, and children's disused pockets,
under wine caskets, under rubble if a dog can go there.

We do not search weasels' mouths, we do follow after mice,
we do not bother with long unopened vaults of business tripe,
we do not search the dead,
we do search their meals if uneaten and saved for no reason.

If the search is interrupted and we know where we left off,
we do not search the same hideaways;
but if we forgot where we were last,
we search bridges and their underflow.

SHE STEPPED

She stepped into mud to the knee,
her leg anchored to the marsh's heart.
Some say she lost her will to walk, though she could.

She never again guided.
Unlike a highway worker dreaming of new detours in the wild,
she had no strength to wave flags.
The mud had sucked on her without resistance,
but men who sought to cling
were flicked off like clods of brittle beef.

Rivers she saw as flat waterfalls,
and the skies over the bog, a pillow's insides.
The very idea of a heron
or a chicory blossom
was a large enclosure of a vague aroma.

AUCTION: FRENCH WINE 1848

Auction: French wine 1848
bottles probably washed in the Seine
stretching on racks to show their bellies
to the usual sniffers and hoteliers;
everyone thrums their auction cards

Why bid
if I'm afraid to drink it;
what quality control over dregs
did they have in wine cellars
soon after Napoleon died;
shaking the bottle
sounds like wash water
splashing a patch of cobblestone
where a carriage just clacked

This was not drinkable even
when Europe had moping monarchies
and vintners thought of joining
the workers' revolts;
cottagers who went to factories
to press berets
thought steam engines
were postmodern
and microbes heretical

That is why each age should drink
its own wine
and each cohort of winemakers
find only passing joy
whenever fruit ferments

I TRAVELLED

I travelled to the border of Ashistan
where even revolutionary clerks squander time.
I found the trackers use the word *higgel* to mean
a large raptor, like an eagle.

On a journey to the heights of Talakal,
where I left large amounts of money and silk thread with widows,
I found the people called small children *kits*.

Lost in the large slum of Fuentalban,
during an unusual sandstorm,
I heard blinded cabbies shouting for more *mun*,
which I took to be cash.

On a freight boat in Gancha
pressed among illegal passengers,
I noticed they called their own sweat *swei*,
but the sweat of others, *peig*,
which was either related to pig,
or beg.

CHRONICLES

I

Perfume-makers are no longer
answering the wind.
Unsung trianglists
have taken over
the musical possibilities of the world.
And in that house
where scribes have been barricaded
for several days,
no written word
can hope to escape alive.

Those entrusted with making the idols
are hypocrites;
after a day of sculpting, pounding,
moulding gods for sale,
they leave for home
with slivers of gold
tucked into their ears
and end canals
where no one would
commit the sacrilege of looking.

In the morning
dulled by one more
week of quotas,
the foreman of trivial gods,
the superintendent of fates,
and the crew in charge of better luck
put away their pagan tools
beneath the mother-breasted tree
where they picket the holy ground
for evidence of a miracle.

II

In the upper hold of a cliff's forehead
mummies gelled or leathered
by time
hidden from tomb robbers
moved from grave to crevice
by devoted priests
in the buried blare
of Egyptological moonlight.

They asked:
are we safe
beneath our gem-studs and bandages
molten in pitch;
are we free to ask the eviscerator,
return our brains and bellies.

Are we entitled
at last
to wear our golden faces
in the sun we have not seen
since death insisted
we come fully dressed.

III

The night has three parts :
in the first, a donkey coughs;
the second, dogs betray each other;
the third, wife and husband talk.

Work, war, love;
slavery, exile, redemption;

three lives that stretch from
sand, moon, to sun,
really one logic
capable of unending blessing
capable of unending night.

HERZL'S BEARD

His beard had its own face.
Its obsession, although not religious,
was to move Jews torn
like a map of Europe,
maybe to Uganda.

He was able to predict his own death,
yet he thought a Rothschild or a Hirsch
would want to pay the sultan
for Palestine.

Did he dream they feared he would write
them into
one of his light plays
about the domestic Viennese
or were worried a spool of tailors
would hold their cuffs in lesser esteem
if they didn't.

An odd-hour king of the Jews,
who gathered the children round the
Xmas tree before he knew better,
flimsier than his wife's histrionics
he could have been transparent
like a Mahler converting for a job
like a Freud thinking through his thighs
like a Dreyfus accusing himself
of not being a better Frenchman or
like any nervous Jew
checking Messiah's watch.

He reached the height of his exiled life
when, waiting in the anteroom for the king,
he realized the size of his nose
and his mastery of German
qualified him to ask for nothing less
than a new geography.

Even so,
none of his children or child's child longed
for a view of Jaffa
from the deck of his steamer.

He died as a royalty should
without notice or excuse.
The bones in his tomb,
even if reburied in home soil
had no capacity to sprout almonds
like Aaron's staff.
That they were lifeless is understood.
That they did not know they would have
rolled anyway through the earth
for the opening night of the Old City's Temple
is best not said on his mountaintop.

ONE THOUSAND YEARS OF JEWISH SPANISH HISTORY

at bar mitzvah lunch
she said she had read
one thousand years of Jewish Spanish history
but could not understand why Jews
from Geronda, Cordova
from Grenada and Toledo,
who lived
under ivied columns and mosaic roses,
who delivered medicines and market advice
to untold viziers
and knew how friendly their neighbours were
should declare they were the chosen people
by the way they ate and lived by themselves.

having just introduced myself,
and needing the tomatoed olives
on the other side of her frilled elbow,
I agreed they were chosen, and had no reason to be otherwise
especially when they blessed the monthly Iberian moon.
but why should we invite calumny if all it takes is a common lunch,
she asked over the waiter's intervening plate.

as a nurse, she could sense the pain
of the *auto-da-fé*
and knew decimations
could not have befallen without provocation
but to throw in Spain's face that we were chosen
made no Mediterranean logic.

I had not finished my plate before the waiter swept clean.
she had gone to chat at the orchid display.
I noticed near the bar
at a table set for unexpected guests
the Torquemada dressed in starched winged collars
had no one to share his lunch,
but seemed all tuckered out from dancing with the men

BEN-YEHUDA'S HEBREW DICTIONARY

While you were sniffing through codices
in the stacks of the great libraries
like an inmate obsessed with keys,
did you notice that the books were stuffed doves
and the buildings squatted on the same *beit*
that introduced the world.

Ordering your wife to speak to your son
only in Hebrew was an act of love,
as was sending her to run for money
when the printer needed faith,
as was converting new syllables into secular needs.

With such love, fanatic to the *tav*,
did you happen to look for Rambam's medicines
or notice stones of the Temple in the towns of Europe
or listen to voices in a mystic's *shul*
or see from the face of your own mirror
that Hebrew shaped the eye
as it did the wisdom of roosters to discern day from night.

And did you notice that
before all dictionaries and their meanings
and all the meant words and the holding of words in scrolls
and all talk and thoughts in talk,
before bodies and cells of souls,
even before here and there, whether in space or outside its crust,
the *aleph beit* skipped so no book could define,
the roots of their phrases grew roots in the land,
the words themselves formed an ideal tongue,
the same tongue found on each child's gums.

YOU HAD ALL THE FREEDOM

You had all the freedom
to take your credit card and coupons
for a ride beyond the mall.

You could have found a hotel for the eager
or substituted for a hat-check girl at a tractorpull.
Maybe you would have befriended a
downbeat accordion player
or seen a lawyer for a class suit.

Yet you chose to return
when the moon was roundest
to see if cabin fever had also driven
me away.

While you were gone, instead of changing a fuse
I could have hitched a ride on a motorcycle
without a headlight,
or done midnight shift at
a rendering plant.
Maybe I would have lain over a steaming
manhole or bathed myself in a prairie plague of locusts.

But like you, I chose to return.
I gave up an offer to sell roadside hubcaps
and scalp season tickets
just to be with you.

THE FAMILY OF WORRIES

The family of worries started with the woman
from beyond many walls
whose son, when angry,
had a donkey's voice.
Her husband never spoke in the sunlight or moonlight;
but all their later children were orators.

The family of joys started with the woman
found in a river blocked to sift out fish.
She dried out for years until her husband
bathed her in a stream of ointments and sauces
that made her light-humoured.
Their children were each doctors of different liquids
like oils and running saps,
so expert they could joke about their molecules.

These families mixed with each other
and with families of bargain-hunters,
of sayers of gratitude, of nostalgia,
of music writers and sword swallowers.
Their progeny had no pure traceable lines
and did not care
until there arose a multisyllabic leader.
He proclaimed his outbursts, his iron tears
and his unused smile wrinkles
were the heritage of the founding matriarch
whose name he had created.

For good reason, he felt his leadership ignored,
and so he became sullen
and married hundreds of shy women
sitting by the telephone.

Today, purely as a generality,
families with long names are descended from worries
and all the rest from joys.

WE CRY OUT

We cry out as a mass of mouths in the streets
not only when dictators have to go.

When it fails to rain for a year,
when buildings tremble over fault lines,
when shrewd animals are free to stalk,
we efface all private tongues,
all backtalk and wit stop running like the trains.

With one great surge of human cells,
in one enormous pulse of air
we blow on the horns for help and cry:
heroes have abandoned us;
the dark and cold prove they have left;
the only clothes we have are what we made up.

JEWEL WEIGENSBERG

Lazar Sarna was born in Montreal, Canada, where he currently practices law. He is the author of the poetry collections *The Singsong* (1968), *Mystics on a Picnic,* Hillel (1972) and *Letters of State,* Porcupine's Quill (1978), as well as a novel *The Man Who Lived Near Nelligan,* Coach House Press (1975). His poetry has appeared in the anthologies *Cross cut,* Vehicule Press (1982) and *Jerusalem,* Vehicule Press (1996), and has been published in *Antigonish Review, Canadian Forum, Canadian Literature, Descant, Fiddlehead* and *Prism International.*